BOSTON COMMON PRESS
Brookline, Massachusetts

2000

Other titles in the *Cook's Illustrated*
How to Cook Series

How to Barbecue and Roast on the Grill
How to Cook Garden Vegetables
How to Cook Holiday Roasts and Birds
How to Cook Shrimp and Other Shellfish
How to Grill
How to Make a Pie
How to Make an American Layer Cake
How to Make Cookie Jar Favorites
How to Make Holiday Desserts
How to Make Ice Cream
How to Make Pasta Sauces
How to Make Pizza
How to Make Pot Pies and Casseroles
How to Make Salad
How to Make Simple Fruit Desserts
How to Sauté
How to Make Soup
How to Make Stew
How to Stir-Fry

HOW TO COOK POTATOES

An illustrated step-by-step guide to perfect potatoes every time.

THE COOK'S ILLUSTRATED LIBRARY

Illustrations by John Burgoyne

Boston Common Press
17 Station Street
Brookline, MA 02445

ISBN 0-936184-42-6
Library of Congress Cataloging-in-Publication Data
The Editors of *Cook's Illustrated*
How to cook potatoes: An illustrated step-by-step guide to perfect potatoes every time./The Editors of *Cook's Illustrated*
1st ed.

Includes 50 recipes and 8 illustrations
ISBN 0-936184-42-6 (hardback): $14.95
I. Cooking. I. Title
2000

Manufactured in the United States of America

Distributed by Boston Common Press, 17 Station Street, Brookline, MA 02445.

Cover and text design: Amy Klee
Recipe development: Elizabeth Germain
Series editor: Jack Bishop

CONTENTS

introduction

LAST SUMMER, I GREW EIGHT DIFFERENT varieties of potatoes in order to test which would grow best in the rocky soil of our Vermont mountain farm. I tried Caribe, Green Mountain, Epicure, and Red Sun as well as some purple and fingerling varieties. What I found surprised me. Green Mountain, the local favorite, grew well, but the Epicure was a bust. Some varieties were starchier than others, but most fell in between the traditional labels of "high starch" and "low starch." In other words, potatoes are both more interesting and more complicated than I had thought. Although most of us have some idea of what is meant by a "baking," "all-purpose," or "new" potato, it turns out that most potatoes are not easily classified.

Our conclusion, then, was that a book devoted entirely to cooking potatoes made sense in an age when we are inclined to move beyond the simple baked potato or the traditional American potato salad. Which oven temperature is best for the perfect baked potato? How does one produce a smooth, lush filling when making twice-baked potatoes? How can roasted potatoes be made crisp on the outside yet creamy and moist on the inside? We also tested the best methods for mashing, frying, boiling, and sautéing potatoes, and we learned how to produce the best hash browns, latkes, and potato gratin.

Of course, there are tens of thousands of potato recipes in cookbooks from all over the world. Our goal was to start with the basics, test them rigorously, and then publish our findings. Once you have mastered the fundamental principles underlying these simple master recipes, you can use them as the basis for countless variations. After you learn how to properly cook and mash potatoes, for example, the possible variations on this dish are, if not limitless, certainly inspiring.

How to Cook Potatoes is the 20th book in the How to Cook Series published by *Cook's Illustrated,* a bimonthly publication on American home cooking. Turn to the beginning of the book for a complete list of titles in the series. To order other books, call us at (800) 611-0759 or visit us online at www.cooksillustrated.com. For a free trial copy of *Cook's,* call (800) 526-8442.

Christopher P. Kimball
Publisher and Editor
Cook's Illustrated

chapter one

POTATO BASICS

THE COOK HAS TWO CHALLENGES WHEN preparing any recipe with potatoes. The first is to determine the best cooking method. How should potatoes be baked? What's the best way to make mashed potatoes? A second question is nearly as important. What kind of potato works best in a specific recipe? While other vegetables in most markets vary by size and freshness, in most cases, shoppers will find only one variety of that vegetable. Broccoli is broccoli, carrots are carrots. Even when there are several varieties (as with heirloom tomatoes), most can be used interchangeably. Yes, one tomato might look a bit different or be a bit sweeter than another, but they are closely related.

With potatoes, this is not the case. Make french fries with Red Bliss potatoes and the fries will be heavy and greasy. Use russet potatoes in salad and they will fall apart into potato mush.

The fact that dozens of potato varieties are grown in this country makes the question of which potato is best for a specific recipe even more confusing. At any time you may see as many as five or six kinds of potatoes in your supermarket. Go to a farmers' market and you may see a dozen varieties. Some potatoes are sold by varietal name (such as Red Bliss or Yukon Gold), but others are sold by generic name (baking, all-purpose, etc.).

STARCH CONTENT

To make sense of this confusion, it is helpful to group potatoes into three major categories based on their ratio of solids (mostly starch) to water. The categories are high-starch/low-moisture potatoes, medium-starch potatoes, and low-starch/high-moisture potatoes.

Each of the recipes in this book has been tested with all three major types of potatoes. In each recipe, we have listed the commonly available variety that works best.

You can safely make substitutions within each category (for example, other varieties of red potato can be used in place of Red Bliss potatoes in salad). Substitutions between categories are more problematic. In a few recipes, such as potato gratin, different potatoes give different results, but all are acceptable. In most cases, however, one type of potato is clearly preferred.

HIGH-STARCH/LOW-MOISTURE POTATOES

Often referred to as baking potatoes, high-starch/low-moisture potatoes can also be used for frying and mashing. The flesh in these potatoes turns dry and fluffy when cooked. Russet potatoes (also called Idaho potatoes) are the most common baking potatoes. Other lesser-known varieties include the All Blue and White Creamer. In all of our recipes, we refer to baking potatoes as russets.

MEDIUM-STARCH POTATOES

These potatoes are considered all-purpose and include Yukon Gold, Yellow Finn, Purple Viking, Caribe, Irish Cobbler, Butterfinger, Ozette, and Purple Peruvian. All-purpose potatoes can be mashed or baked but are generally not as fluffy as the high-starch potatoes. Likewise, they can be boiled for salad, but they won't hold their shape as well as red potatoes. We generally recommend medium-starch potatoes in recipes for dishes such as home fries, where a combination of these traits is desirable.

LOW-STARCH/HIGH-MOISTURE POTATOES

This category covers all red-skinned potatoes, including Red Bliss, Red Pontiac, All Red, Dark Red Norland, Ruby Crescent, and Red Creamer. It also includes most new potatoes (see below) as well as the Rose Finn Apple, the Russian Banana, and the White Rose potato. All of these potatoes, often called waxy potatoes, hold their shape better than other potatoes when sliced or diced and cooked. They are best roasted, sautéed, or boiled and used in salad.

STORAGE POTATOES VERSUS NEW POTATOES

In addition to categorizing potatoes by starch content, it is useful to divide them into two groups based on how they have been handled after harvesting.

STORAGE POTATOES

Most potatoes are cured after harvesting to toughen their skins and protect their flesh. They are then held in cold storage, often for months. These potatoes are called storage potatoes. Almost all of the potatoes in supermarkets are storage potatoes.

NEW POTATOES

Occasionally potatoes are harvested before they have developed their full complement of starch. New potatoes are always waxy (low in starch, high in moisture), even if they are actually a high-starch variety. Although all new potatoes are small, not all small potatoes are new. You can pick out a new potato by examining the skin. If the skin feels thin and you can rub it off with your fingers, you are holding a new potato. New potatoes have a lot of moisture and their flesh is almost juicy when cut.

SWEET POTATOES

Finally, there is the sweet potato. This tuber is in fact not a potato at all. It is part of the morning glory family. The kind of sweet potato found in most markets is orange-fleshed (they are labeled yams but are not related to the tropical plant of that name), but yellow-fleshed varieties are available in some markets. For more information on buying and cooking sweet potatoes, see chapter 12.

KEEPING POTATOES AT HOME

Since potatoes seem almost indestructible compared with other vegetables, little thought is generally given to their storage. But because various problems can result from inadequate storage conditions, we decided to find out how much difference storage really makes. We stored all-purpose potatoes in five environments: in a cool (50–60 degrees Fahrenheit), dark place; in the refrigerator; in a basket near a sunlit window; in a warm (70–80 degrees), dark place; and in a drawer with some onions at room temperature. We checked all the potatoes after four weeks.

As expected, the potatoes stored in the cool, dark place were firm, had not sprouted, and were crisp and moist when cut. There were no negative marks on the potatoes stored in the refrigerator, either. Although some experts say that the sugar level dramatically increases in some potato varieties under these conditions, we could not see or taste any difference between these potatoes and the ones stored in the cool, dark but unrefrigerated environment.

Our last three storage tests produced unfavorable results. The potatoes stored in sunlight, in warm storage, and with onions at room temperature developed a greenish tinge. When potatoes are stressed by improper storage, the level of naturally occurring toxins increases, causing the greenish tinge known as *solanine.* Because solanine is not destroyed during cooking, any part of the potato with this greenish coloring should be completely cut away before cooking.

The skin of the potatoes stored in sunlight became gray and mottled, while the potatoes stored in a warm place and those stored with onions sprouted and became soft and wrinkled. Sprouts also contain increased levels of solanine and should be cut away before cooking.

chapter two

BAKED POTATOES

TO CONFIRM THE GENERAL WISDOM ON what constitutes the best baking potato, we baked an all-purpose potato, Yukon Gold, and the standard baking potato, russet, and found that russets do produce the fluffiest and—to our mind—the best baked potato. We baked russets at temperatures ranging from 350 to 500 degrees and discovered that traditional slow baking is best, mainly because of the effect it has on the skin. The skin of a potato baked at 350 degrees for an hour and 15 minutes simply has no peer. Just under the skin, a well-baked potato will develop a substantial brown layer. This is because the dark skin absorbs heat during cooking, and the starch just inside the skin is broken down into sugar and starts to brown. If you love baked potato skin, this is definitely the best method.

If slow baking is essential to good skin, the consistency of the flesh also requires some attention. Letting the potato sit awhile after baking without opening it up will steam the potato and cause the flesh to become more dense. For fluffy potatoes, create a wide opening to let steam escape as soon as the potatoes come out of the oven.

Twice-baked potatoes are essentially baked potatoes from which the flesh has been removed, mashed with dairy ingredients and seasonings, mounded back in the shells, and baked again. This dish offers a good range of both texture and flavor in a single morsel. Done well, the skin is chewy and substantial without being tough, with just a hint of crispness to play off the smooth, creamy filling. In terms of flavor, cheese and other dairy ingredients make the filling rich and tangy, a contrast with the potato's mild, slightly sweet shell.

Because twice-baked potatoes are put in the oven twice, we found it best to limit the initial baking to an hour, rather than the usual 75 minutes. Oiling the skins before baking and using a higher oven temperature promote crispness—not something you necessarily want in plain baked potatoes but a trait we came to admire in creamy twice-baked potatoes. Another difference in the treatment of baked and twice-baked potatoes occurs when they come out of the oven. Unlike baked potatoes, which should be cut open immediately to release steam, twice-baked potatoes should be allowed to sit and cool down a bit, which makes them easier to handle. Because the flesh is mixed with wet ingredients, any compromise to the texture from unreleased moisture is negligible.

Once the potato halves had been emptied of their flesh, they got a little flabby sitting on the counter waiting to be stuffed. Because the oven was still on and waiting for the return of the stuffed halves, we decided to put the skins back in while we prepared the filling. That worked beautifully, giving the shells an extra dimension of crispness.

Pleased with our chewy, slightly crunchy skins, we now had to develop a smooth, lush, flavorful filling. Dozens of further tests helped us refine our filling to a rich, but not killer, combination of sharp cheddar, sour cream, buttermilk, and butter. We learned to season the filling aggressively with salt and pepper; for herbs, the slightly sharp flavor of scallions or chives was best.

With the filling mixed and mounded back into the shells, our last tests centered on the final baking. We wanted to do more than just heat the filling through; we intended to form an attractive brown crust on it as well. We found that using the broiler was the was easiest and most effective method. After 10 or 15 minutes, the potatoes emerged browned, crusted, and ready for the table.

Master Recipe

Baked Potatoes

serves 4

NOTE: *We found that no benefit or harm was done to the potatoes by poking them with the tines of a fork before putting them in the oven. Do use a fork to open the skin as soon as the potatoes come out of the oven (see figures 1 and 2, page 18). Season with salt to taste and a pat of butter. If you like, embellish with a dollop of sour cream, crumbled bacon, grated or shredded cheese, or minced chives or scallions.*

4 medium russet potatoes (7 to 8 ounces each), scrubbed

INSTRUCTIONS:

1. Preheat oven to 350 degrees. Place potatoes on middle rack and bake until skewer glides easily through flesh, about 75 minutes.

2. Remove potatoes from oven and pierce with a fork to create a dotted X (see figure 1, page 18). Press in at ends of potato to push flesh up and out (see figure 2, page 18). Season as desired and serve immediately.

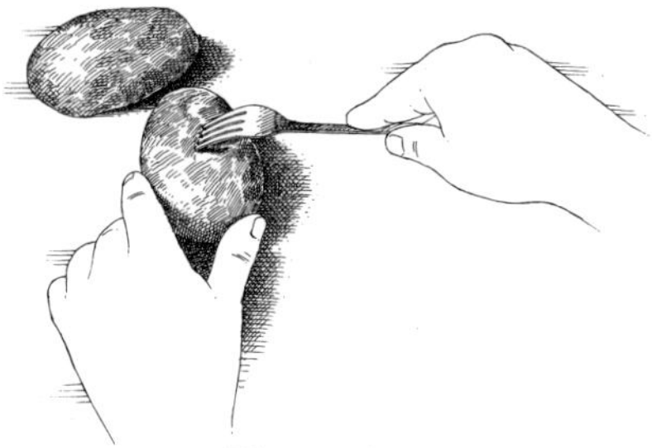

Figure 1.
Use the tines of a fork to make a dotted X on top of each baked potato.

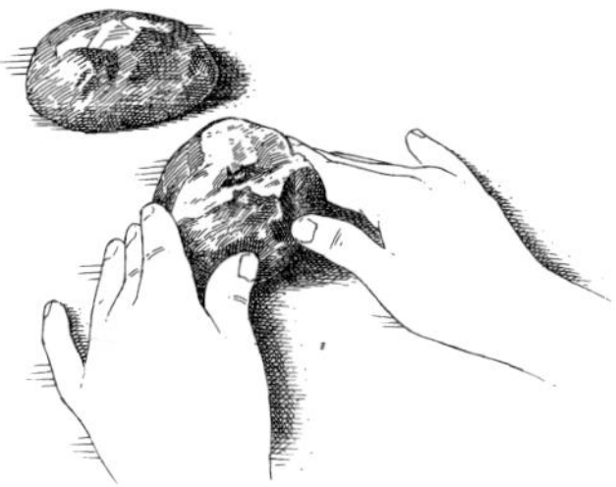

Figure 2.
Press in at the ends of the potato to push the flesh up and out. This method maximizes the amount of steam released and creates the fluffiest texture. In addition, we find that butter tends to slide right out of potatoes that are slit lengthwise. With the flesh pushed up this way, the potato does a better job of holding onto the butter. The butter thus ends up in the potato and not on your plate.

Quicker Baked Potatoes

serves 4

➢ NOTE: *This half-and-half method produces far superior results than straight microwaving. By the time you have scrubbed the potatoes and microwaved them, the oven will be preheated. To cook fewer potatoes by this method, plan on 2 minutes total cooking time in the microwave for each potato. Don't try to microwave more than four potatoes at one time.*

4 medium russet potatoes (7 to 8 ounces each), scrubbed

INSTRUCTIONS:

1. Preheat oven to 450 degrees. Place 4 scrubbed potatoes in microwave and cook at high power for 4 minutes. Turn potatoes over and cook at high power for another 4 minutes.

2. Transfer potatoes to hot oven and cook until skewer glides easily through flesh, about 20 minutes. Open as directed in figures 1 and 2 (page 18), and serve immediately.

Master Recipe

Twice-Baked Potatoes

serves 6 to 8

➢ NOTE: *To vary the flavor a bit, try substituting other types of cheese, such as Gruyère, fontina, or feta, for the cheddar. Yukon Gold potatoes, though slightly more moist than our ideal, gave our twice-baked potatoes a buttery flavor and mouthfeel that everyone liked, so we recommend them as a substitution for the russets.*

- 4 medium russet potatoes (7 to 8 ounces each), scrubbed, dried, and rubbed lightly with vegetable oil
- 4 ounces sharp cheddar cheese, shredded (about 1 cup)
- ½ cup sour cream
- ½ cup buttermilk
- 2 tablespoons unsalted butter, softened
- 3 medium scallions, sliced thin
- ½ teaspoon salt
- Ground black pepper

INSTRUCTIONS:

1. Adjust oven rack to upper-middle position and heat oven to 400 degrees. Bake potatoes on foil-lined baking sheet until skin is crisp and deep brown and skewer easily pierces flesh, about 1 hour. Setting baking sheet aside, transfer potatoes to wire rack and let sit until cool enough to handle, about 10 minutes.

2. Using an oven mitt or folded kitchen towel to handle hot potatoes, cut each potato in half so that long, blunt side rests on work surface (see figure 3, page 23). Using a small dinner spoon, scoop flesh from each half into medium bowl, leaving a ⅛-inch to ¼-inch thickness of flesh in each shell. Arrange shells on lined sheet and return to oven until dry and slightly crisped, about 10 minutes. Meanwhile, mash potato flesh with fork until smooth. Stir in remaining ingredients, including pepper to taste, until well combined.

3. Remove shells from oven and increase oven setting to broil. Holding shells steady on pan with oven mitt or towel-protected hand, spoon mixture into crisped shells, mounding slightly at the center, and return to oven. Broil until spotty brown and crisp on top, 10 to 15 minutes. Allow to cool for 10 minutes. Serve warm.

VARIATIONS:

Twice-Baked Potatoes with Pepperjack Cheese and Bacon

Fry 8 strips (about 8 ounces) bacon, cut crosswise into ¼-inch pieces, in medium skillet over medium heat until crisp, 5 to 7 minutes. Remove bacon to drain on plate lined with paper towel; set aside. Follow recipe for Twice-Baked Potatoes, substituting pepperjack cheese for cheddar and stirring reserved bacon into filling mixture.

Twice-Baked Potatoes with Chipotle Pepper and Onion

Heat 2 tablespoons butter in medium skillet over medium heat; sauté 1 medium onion, chopped fine, until soft, 3 to 4 minutes, and set aside. Follow recipe for Twice-Baked Potatoes, omitting butter and adding 1 to 1½ tablespoons minced canned chipotle peppers in adobo sauce, reserved sautéed onion, and 2 tablespoons chopped fresh cilantro leaves to filling mixture.

Twice-Baked Potatoes with Smoked Salmon and Chives

This variation makes a fine brunch dish.

Follow recipe for Twice-Baked Potatoes, omitting cheese and scallions and stirring 4 ounces smoked salmon, cut into

½-inch pieces, and 3 tablespoons minced fresh chives into filling mixture. Sprinkle finished potatoes with additional chopped chives as garnish just before serving.

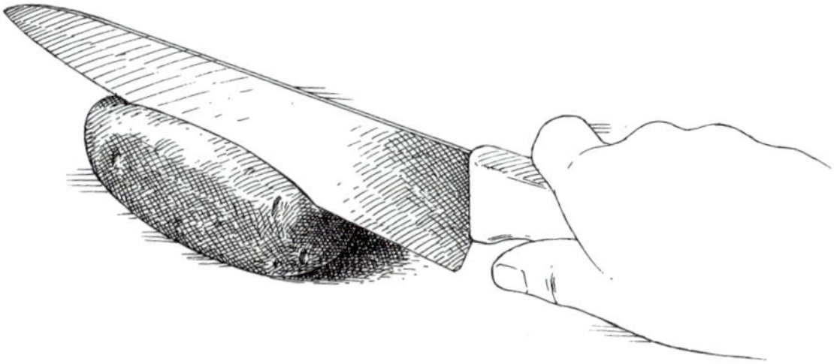

Figure 3.
Most russet potatoes have two relatively flat, blunt sides and two curved sides. Halve the baked potatoes lengthwise so the blunt sides are down once the shells are stuffed, making them much more stable on the pan during the final baking.

chapter three

ROASTED POTATOES

THE PERFECT ROASTED POTATO IS CRISP and deep golden brown on the outside, with moist, velvety, dense interior flesh. The potato's slightly bitter skin is intact, providing a contrast with the sweet, caramelized flavor that the flesh develops during the roasting process. It is rich but never greasy, and it is often accompanied by the heady taste of garlic and herbs.

To start, we roasted several kinds of potatoes. We liked high-starch/low-moisture potatoes (we used russets) the least. They did not brown well, their dry, fluffy texture was more like baked than roasted potatoes, and their flavor reminded us of raw potatoes. Medium-starch all-purpose potatoes (we used Yukon Golds) produced a beautiful golden crust, but the interior flesh was still rather dry. The best roasted potatoes came from the low-starch/high-moisture category (we used Red Bliss). These potatoes emerged from the oven with a light, delicate crust and a moist, dense interior that had a more complex, nutty flavor than the others, with hints of bitterness and tang.

After choosing the Red Bliss potatoes, we began to test oven temperatures. At 425 degrees, the result was an even-colored, golden-brown potato with a thin, crisp crust and an interior that was soft and dense, although still slightly dry.

While researching, we came across some recipes that called for parboiling the potatoes before roasting them. Hoping that this approach would produce a texturally superior potato that retained more of its moisture after cooking, we tried boiling the potatoes for seven minutes prior to roasting. This produced a potato closer to our ideal.

We then tried covering the potatoes for a portion of their roasting time. We were especially drawn to this technique because it allowed the potatoes to steam in their own moisture with little extra effort required on the part of the cook. The results were perfect. The crisp, deep golden-brown crust was perfectly balanced by a creamy, moist interior. These potatoes had a sweet and nutty caramelized flavor, with just a hint of tang from the skin. A very simple method had produced the very best potatoes.

The next step in the process was to figure out how to add garlic flavor, which makes a good variation on standard roasted potatoes. If we added minced garlic during the last five minutes of cooking, it burned almost instantly; coating the potatoes with garlic-infused oil failed to produce the strong garlic flavor we were after; and roasting whole, unpeeled garlic cloves alongside the potatoes and squeezing the pulp out afterward to add to the potatoes was tedious. The best method turned out to be both simple and flavorful: mash raw garlic into a paste, place it in a large stainless steel bowl, put the hot roast potatoes into the bowl, and toss. This method yields potatoes with a strong garlic flavor yet without the raw spiciness of uncooked garlic.

Master Recipe

Roasted Potatoes

serves 4

NOTE: *To roast more than 2 pounds of potatoes at once, use a second pan rather than crowding the first. If your potatoes are as small as new potatoes, cut them in halves instead of wedges and turn them cut-side up during the final 10 minutes of roasting.*

2 pounds Red Bliss or other low-starch potatoes, scrubbed, dried, halved, and cut into ¾-inch wedges

3 tablespoons extra-virgin olive oil

Salt and ground black pepper

INSTRUCTIONS:

1. Adjust oven rack to middle position and heat oven to 425 degrees. Toss potatoes and oil in medium bowl to coat; season generously with salt and pepper to taste and toss again to blend.

2. Place potatoes flesh-side down in a single layer on shallow roasting pan; cover tightly with aluminum foil and cook for 20 minutes. Remove foil; roast until side of potato touching pan is crusty golden brown, about 15 minutes more.

3. Remove pan from oven and carefully turn potatoes over using metal spatula (see figure 4, page 29). Return pan to oven and roast until side of potato now touching pan is crusty golden brown and skins have raisinlike wrinkles, 5 to 10 minutes more. Remove from oven, transfer potatoes to serving dish (again, using metal spatula and extra care not to rip crusts), and serve immediately.

VARIATIONS:

Roasted Potatoes with Garlic and Rosemary

While potatoes are roasting, mince 2 medium garlic cloves; sprinkle with ⅛ teaspoon salt and mash with flat side of chef's knife blade until paste forms. Transfer garlic paste to large bowl; set aside. In last 3 minutes of roasting time, sprinkle 2 tablespoons chopped fresh rosemary evenly over potatoes. Immediately transfer potatoes to bowl with garlic, toss, and serve.

Roasted Potatoes with Garlic, Feta, Olives, and Oregano

While potatoes are roasting, mince 2 medium garlic cloves; sprinkle with ⅛ teaspoon salt and mash with flat side of chef's knife blade until paste forms. Transfer garlic paste to large bowl; add ½ cup crumbled feta cheese, 12 pitted and chopped kalamata olives, and 1 tablespoon lemon juice; set aside. In last 3 minutes of roasting time, sprinkle 2 tablespoons chopped fresh oregano evenly over potatoes. Immediately transfer potatoes to bowl with garlic mixture, toss, and serve.

Roasted Potatoes with Spicy Caramelized Onions

While potatoes are roasting, heat medium skillet over medium-high heat. Add 2 tablespoons olive oil and 1 medium onion, halved and sliced thin, and salt and ground black pepper to taste. Reduce heat to medium and cook, stirring occasionally, until onions are caramelized and deep golden brown, about 15 minutes. Stir in ¼ teaspoon cayenne pepper and 1 teaspoon ground cumin; cook until fragrant, about 1 minute longer. Transfer to large bowl; add 1½ teaspoons lime juice, 2 tablespoons chopped fresh parsley, and roasted potatoes. Toss and serve.

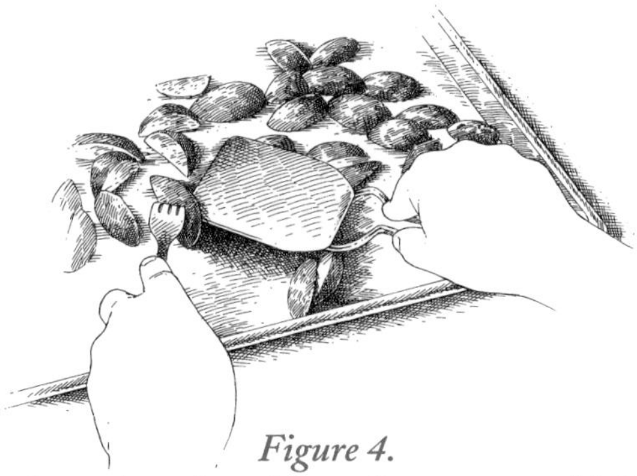

Figure 4.

Press the metal spatula against roasting pan as you slide it under the potatoes to protect the crisp crust. Flip the potatoes so that the other cut sides come into contact with the hot pan.

chapter four

MASHED POTATOES

POTATOES ARE COMPOSED MOSTLY OF STARCH and water. The starch is in the form of granules, which in turn are contained in starch cells. The higher the starch content of the potato, the fuller the cells. In high-starch potatoes, the cells are completely full—they look like plump little beach balls. In medium- and low-starch potatoes, the cells are more like underinflated beach balls. The space between these less-than-full cells is taken up mostly by water.

In our tests, we found that the full starch cells of high-starch potatoes are most likely to maintain their integrity and stay separate when mashed, giving the potatoes a delightfully fluffy texture. In addition, the low water content of these potatoes allows them to absorb milk, cream, and/or butter without becoming wet or gummy. Starch cells in lower-starch potatoes, on the other hand, tend to clump when cooked and break more easily, allowing the starch to dissolve into whatever liquid is present. The broken cells and dissolved starch make for gummy mashed potatoes.

Conventional recipes call for boiling large chunks of peeled potatoes. Knowing that the skin can keep potatoes from becoming water-logged when boiled, we wondered what would happen if we peeled the potatoes after boiling.

When we boiled whole russet potatoes with their skins on, then peeled and mashed them, the results were fantastic. The mashed potatoes had a stronger potato flavor and the texture was smoother. By comparison, potatoes cooked the conventional way (peeled and cut into chunks) were watery tasting and a bit grainy.

Potatoes boiled with their skins on were also much drier after ricing or mashing. As a result, they could absorb much more dairy and butter than conventionally cooked potatoes. The result is the richest, most delicious mashed potatoes ever. While it is a bit of a pain to peel hot boiled potatoes, we think the results justify this minor inconvenience.

We prefer to force cooked potatoes through a food mill, which turns the potatoes into fine, thin shreds. With the potatoes already mashed, you can blend in milk and butter with a rubber spatula, which is gentle on those starch cells and therefore helps ensure consistently fluffy mashed potatoes. While a ricer works just as well as a food mill, it is less convenient; the container that holds the potatoes is fairly small, so you need to cut the hot potatoes in half.

The more traditional mashers are usually of two types: a disk with large holes in it or a curvy wire loop. We found the disk to be more efficient for reducing both mashing time and the number of lumps in the finished product. (Potatoes mashed in this way, however, will never be silky, as are those put through a food mill or ricer.) If you choose a masher, don't use a spatula to blend in the other ingredients, as recommended with the food mill and ricer, but blend and mash at the same time to minimize stickiness.

Many recipes call for heating milk before adding it, justifying this by saying that cold milk makes mashed potatoes sticky. Our repeated experiments have demonstrated that this is not true. Cold milk does cool the potatoes, which you really don't want. Our choice is to use warm milk, but only because it keeps the potatoes up to temperature. While you can certainly use milk to make mashed potatoes, our tasters preferred versions made with half-and-half, which gives mashed potatoes a richer mouthfeel and flavor. If you insist on using milk, whole milk is superior to low-fat milk.

Master Recipe

Mashed Potatoes

serves 4

NOTE: *Russet potatoes make slightly fluffier mashed potatoes, but Yukon Golds have an appealing buttery flavor and can be used if you prefer. Mashed potatoes stiffen and become gluey as they cool, so they are best served piping hot. If you must hold mashed potatoes before serving, place them in a heatproof bowl, cover the bowl tightly with plastic wrap, and set the bowl over a pot of simmering water. The potatoes will remain hot and soft-textured for one hour.*

2 pounds russet potatoes, scrubbed
1 cup half-and-half, warmed
4 tablespoons unsalted butter, softened and cut into 4 equal pieces
Salt and ground black pepper

INSTRUCTIONS:

1. Place potatoes in large saucepan with cold water to cover (about 2 quarts). Bring to a boil over high heat, reduce heat, and simmer, covered, until potatoes are just tender when pricked with a thin-bladed knife, about 20 minutes.

2. Peel potatoes by holding in a clean kitchen towel folded twice and using a paring knife to peel skin. Drop them one at a time, cut in half if necessary, into a food mill or ricer and process them back into warm, dry saucepan. (If you don't mind some lumps, drop peeled potatoes back into warm, dry saucepan and mash with potato masher.) Using a rubber spatula, add half-and-half and salt to taste. Add butter, continue to mix until melted. Season generously with pepper and serve hot.

VARIATIONS:

Mashed Potatoes with Parmesan and Lemon

Stir in 1 cup grated Parmesan cheese, after adding half-and-half but before adding butter. Add butter, then stir in minced or grated zest from 2 lemons.

Mashed Potatoes with Pesto

We find it best to use pesto made with half parsley so that the heat of the potatoes doesn't turn the pesto army green.

Place ¼ cup toasted pine nuts, walnuts, or almonds, 1 peeled garlic clove, 1 cup fresh basil leaves, 1 cup fresh parsley leaves, and 7 tablespoons extra-virgin olive oil in workbowl of food processor; process until smooth, stopping as necessary to scrape down sides of bowl. Transfer mixture to small bowl, stir in ¼ cup grated Parmesan cheese, and add salt to taste. Add pesto to the mashed potatoes in place of butter.

Mashed Potatoes with Root Vegetables

Most root vegetables are more watery than potatoes, so you will need less than the full cup of half-and-half.

Replace 1 pound of potatoes with 1 pound of parsnips, rutabagas, celery root, carrots, or turnips that have been peeled and cut into 1½- to 2-inch chunks. Add half-and-half ¼ cup at a time until the desired consistency is obtained.

Mashed Potatoes with Garlic and Olive Oil

Add 6 to 8 peeled garlic cloves to saucepan with potatoes in step 1. Replace butter with ¼ cup extra-virgin olive oil.

Buttermilk Mashed Potatoes

Buttermilk gives mashed potatoes a pleasing tang and rich texture, even when less butter is used. If you are interested in mashed potatoes with less fat, this is your best option.

Replace half-and-half with 1 cup warmed buttermilk. Reduce butter to 1 tablespoon.

chapter five

FRIED POTATOES

THE IDEAL FRENCH FRY IS LONG AND CRISP, with sides cut at right angles, a nice crunch on the outside, and an earthy potato taste. Its bass flavor note should be rustic, like a mushroom's, and its high note should hint of the oil in which it was cooked. It should definitely not droop, and its coloring should be two-toned, blond with hints of brown.

Obviously, a good french fry requires the right potato. Would it be starchy or waxy? We tested two of the most popular waxy potatoes, and neither was even close to ideal. During frying, their abundance of water evaporated, leaving hollows inside the potato that filled with oil. The finished fries were greasy. Next we tested the starchy potato most readily available nationwide, the russet. This potato turned out to be ideal, frying up with all the qualities we were looking for.

Because russets are starchy, it is important to rinse the starch off the surface after cutting the potato into fries. To do this, simply put the cut fries in a bowl, place the bowl in the sink, and run cold water into it, swirling with your fingers until the water runs clear. This might seem like an unimportant step, but it makes a real difference. When we skipped the starch rinse, the fries weren't quite right, and the oil clouded.

At this point, you take the second crucial step: Fill the bowl with clear water, add ice, and refrigerate the potatoes for at least 30 minutes. That way, when the potatoes first enter the hot oil, they are nearly frozen; this allows a slow, thorough cooking of the inner potato pulp. When we tried making fries without chilling them first, the outsides started to brown well before the insides were fully cooked.

Our preference is to peel potatoes for french fries. A skin-on fry does not form those little airy blisters, which we like. Peeling the potato also allows the cook to see—and remove—any imperfections or greenish coloring.

What is the right fat for making perfect french fries? To find out, we experimented with lard, vegetable shortening, canola oil, corn oil, and peanut oil. Lard and shortening make great fries, but we figured that for health reasons many cooks won't want to use these products. We moved on to canola oil, but we were unhappy with the results: bland, almost watery fries.

Corn oil was the most forgiving oil in the test kitchen. It rebounded well from temperature fluctuations, and it held up very well when the same oil was used for several batches of fries. What's more, the fries tasted marvelous. Peanut oil also produced good results. A potato fried in peanut oil is light, and the flavor is rich but not dense. The earthy flavor of the potato is there, as with corn oil, but is not overbearing. At this point, we were very close, but something was still missing. The high flavor note, which is supplied by the animal fat in lard, was lacking.

We tried a dollop of strained bacon grease in peanut oil, about two generous tablespoons per quart of oil. The meaty flavor came through, but without its nasty baggage.

So bacon grease appeared to be the animal fat of choice. To be certain of this, we added bacon grease to each of the oils, with these results: canola oil, extra body, but still short on flavor; corn oil, more body, more flavor, nearly perfect; peanut oil, flavor, bite, body, bass notes, high notes galore. At last, an equivalent to lard.

So now it was time to get down to the frying, which actually means double-frying. First, we fried the potatoes at a relatively low temperature to release their rich and earthy flavor. Then we quick-fried them at a higher temperature until they were nicely browned and served them immediately.

For the sake of convenience, we also attempted a single, longer frying. Like many cooks before us, we found that with standard french fries (as opposed to the much thinner shoestring fries), we could not both sear the outside and properly cook the inside in a single visit to the hot fat. When we left them in long enough to sear the outside, we wound up with wooden, overcooked fries.

We found it easy to adapt our recipe for steak fries. In this case, we like to leave the skin on for a more rustic appearance (although it can be removed) and cut the fries into lengths ½ inch thick. Frying was exactly the same except that steak fries need a couple of extra minutes on the first frying to color.

Oven fries are a completely different animal. Many cooks don't want to deep-fry because of health concerns. They also don't like the mess associated with deep frying. Recipes for oven-fried potatoes have been popular in recent years, but we had found most oven fries to be a pale imitation of the real thing. We wanted fries that were crisp and golden brown. In addition, the inside had to be fluffy and potatoey tasting.

We first experimented with different ways of cutting the potatoes. We assumed that wedges of some sort would work best. However, because the thickness varies (the ends are thinner, the middle quite thick), we found that wedges cook and color unevenly. We had far better luck when we cut the fries into uniform ½-inch-thick lengths, just as we did for steak fries.

As with fries cooked in oil, many sources suggest refrigerating or chilling the raw, cut potatoes in ice water to get oven fries to brown nicely. We found that chilled fries emerged from the oven with a mushy interior and that they were less crisp than potatoes simply cut and oven-fried.

At this point, we wondered if the double-cooking method used with french fries could be adapted to oven fries. We tried steaming the potatoes first, hoping this would set the starches in the fries and help the exterior to crisp up. The potatoes emerged from the steamer quite sticky because of the starches that had been released. We carefully dried the potatoes with a tea towel (they stuck to paper towels) and spread them out in a single layer over a preheated pan.

The fries emerged from the oven crisp and delicious. By getting the potatoes to release some of their starch during steaming, they release less starch in the oven, which allows the exterior to become especially crisp and golden brown.

Master Recipe

French Fries

serves 4

➢ NOTE: *For those who like it, flavoring the oil with a few tablespoons of bacon grease adds a subtle, meaty flavor to the fries. Their texture, however, is not affected if the bacon grease is omitted.*

- **2 pounds russet potatoes, peeled and cut into lengths ¼ by ¼ inch thick** **(see figure 5, page 43)**
- **2 quarts peanut oil**
- **4 tablespoons strained bacon grease (optional)**
- **3 large brown paper bags**
- **Salt and ground black pepper**

INSTRUCTIONS:

1. Rinse cut fries in large bowl under cold running water until water turns from milky colored to clear. Cover with at least 1 inch of water, then cover with ice. Refrigerate at least 30 minutes. (Can be refrigerated up to 3 days ahead.)

2. In 5-quart pot or Dutch oven fitted with clip-on-the-pot candy thermometer, or in large electric fryer, heat oil over medium-low heat to 325 degrees. As oil heats, add bacon grease. Oil will bubble up when you add fries, so be sure you have at least 3 inches of room at top of cooking pot.

3. Pour off ice and water, quickly wrap potatoes in a clean tea towel, and thoroughly pat dry. Increase heat to medium-high and add half of fries, a handful at a time, to hot oil. Fry, stirring with Chinese skimmer or slotted spoon with large holes, until potatoes are limp and soft and start to turn from white to blond, 6 to 8 minutes. (Oil temperature will drop 50 to 60 degrees during this frying.) Use skimmer or slotted spoon to transfer fries to brown paper bag; spread out on bag to drain. Fry remaining potatoes and drain on second bag. Let fries rest at least 10 minutes. (Can stand at room temperature up to 2 hours.)

4. When ready to serve fries, reheat oil to 375 degrees. Using paper bag as a funnel, pour potatoes from one bag into hot oil. Discard bag and open a clean bag on counter. Fry potatoes, stirring fairly constantly, until golden brown and puffed, 2 to 3 minutes. Transfer to open paper bag. Fry remaining potatoes and add to new bag with other fries. Season to taste with salt and pepper or other seasoned salt, close bag, and shake well so bag absorbs excess oil and fries are coated evenly with seasonings. Remove fries from bag and serve immediately.

VARIATIONS:

Spicy Fries

Combine 1 teaspoon chili powder, 1 teaspoon sweet paprika, ½ teaspoon ground cumin, and ⅛ to ¼ teaspoon cayenne pepper in small bowl. Use this mixture in place of black pepper (and with salt) in step 4.

Steak Fries

Peel potatoes or scrub well and leave peels on. Cut into lengths ½ by ½ inch thick. Proceed as directed in recipe for french fries, increasing frying time in step 3 to 10 minutes.

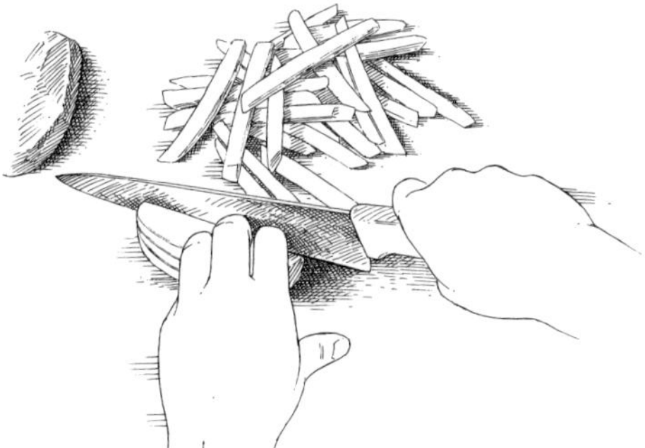

Figure 5.

For standard fries, slice peeled potatoes lengthwise into ovals about ¼ inch thick. Stack several ovals on top of each other and slice them into ¼-inch thick lengths.

Master Recipe

Oven Fries

serves 4

NOTE: *Like french fries, oven fries are twice-cooked for the best texture. First, they are steamed to cook the interior partially and set the starch. Next, they are baked in a hot oven until the exterior is crisp. Make sure to preheat the greased baking sheets as directed. Adding the steamed potatoes to a hot pan makes a difference. There's no need to turn fries. The bottom becomes especially crisp, while the other sides turn golden brown.*

4 teaspoons peanut oil

2 pounds russet potatoes, scrubbed and cut into lengths ½ by ½ inch thick

Salt and ground black pepper

INSTRUCTIONS:

1. Put ½ teaspoon oil on each of two rimmed baking sheets. Use paper towel to spread oil evenly over entire surface, and place both sheets in oven. Preheat oven to 450 degrees. Rinse cut fries in large bowl under cold running water until water turns from milky colored to clear.

2. Fit large pot or Dutch oven with steamer basket; fill with enough water to reach just below bottom of basket. Bring water to boil over high heat; add potatoes to basket. Cover and steam for 5 minutes, until potatoes are glistening but still very firm. Remove potatoes and spread out in single layer on two clean tea towels. Pat dry using a third tea towel.

3. Toss potatoes and remaining tablespoon of oil in medium bowl to coat; season generously with salt and pepper to taste and toss again to blend. Carefully remove one baking sheet from oven and place half of potatoes on baking sheet so they are spread out and not touching each other. Place baking sheet back in oven and repeat process using second baking sheet and remaining potatoes.

4. Bake until potatoes are deep golden brown and have begun to puff, 25 to 30 minutes. Serve immediately.

VARIATIONS:

Oven Fries with Indian Spices

Combine 1 teaspoon ground turmeric, 1 teaspoon ground coriander, ½ teaspoon ground cumin, and 1½ teaspoons curry powder in small bowl. Add spice mixture to steamed potatoes along with salt and pepper in step 3.

Oven Fries with Cheese

Replace pepper in step 3 with 1 teaspoon sweet paprika. When potatoes are done, pull all fries close together on one baking sheet, sprinkle evenly with ¼ cup grated Parmesan cheese, and return to oven until cheese melts, about 1 minute. Serve immediately.

chapter six

POTATO SALAD

POTATO SALADS COME IN NUMEROUS STYLES. Though recipes may seem dramatically different, most have four things in common—potatoes, of course; fat (usually bacon, olive oil, or mayonnaise); an acidic ingredient, usually vinegar, to perk things up; and flavorings for distinction. Though these salads may be very different in character, the issues affecting all of them, it turns out, are much the same.

We first wanted to know what type of potato should be used and how should it be cooked. Recipe writers seemed split down the middle between starchy and waxy potatoes, with starchy praised for being more absorbent and waxy admired for their sturdiness. We have always just boiled potatoes with the skin on, but steaming, microwaving, roasting, and baking are all options.

Next, when should the potato be peeled? On the assumption that hot potatoes are more absorbent, some thought it worth scorching fingertips to get the cooked potatoes peeled and cut immediately. Other recipe writers were more casual—"peel when cool enough to handle." Still others instructed us to refrigerate the cooled potatoes, then peel and cut the next day. And, of course, you may wonder whether you really need to peel them at all.

Finally, should potatoes be seasoned when still warm, assuming that they do absorb flavorings better in this state? Is it worth the two-step process of seasoning the potatoes with vinegar (or vinaigrette), salt, and pepper first? Or should you toss everything together at the same time?

After boiling, steaming, baking/roasting, and microwaving four different varieties of potatoes—Red Bliss, russets, potatoes labeled "all-purpose" in the market, and Yukon Golds—we found Red Bliss to be the potato of choice and boiling the cooking method of choice. Higher-starch potatoes—russets, all-purpose, and Yukon Golds—are not sturdy enough for salads. They fell apart when cut and looked sloppy in salad form.

Before giving up on high-starch potatoes, though, we

wanted to test their absorption power, a selling point for many cooks. A number of potato salad recipes suggested an initial drizzling of vinegar over warm or hot salad potatoes to make them taste seasoned from within as well as dressed from without.

We found that high-starch potatoes are indeed more absorbent than the lower-starch varieties—to a fault. When tossed with vinegar, the high-starch potato salads tasted dry, sucking up all the vinegar and asking for more. These mealy, high-starch potatoes, we determined, were great for mashing or baking, but not for salad. The low-starch boiling potatoes successfully absorbed the vinegar but still remained firm and creamy.

Next we wanted to see if we could boost flavor at the cooking stage by boiling the potatoes in chicken broth and in water heavily seasoned with bay leaves and garlic cloves. The chicken stock may as well have been water—there wasn't even a hint of evidence that the potatoes had been cooked in stock. The bay leaves and garlic smelled wonderful as the potatoes cooked, but the potatoes were still bland-tasting (although the skins smelled faintly of garlic).

We tried boiling potatoes without the skin, but they were waterlogged compared with their skin-on counterparts. In salad form all the potatoes had a sloppy, broken look, and they tasted watery.

Although we might not want to eat the skin of a boiled Idaho in a salad, we found the paper-thin skin of the boiled red potato not unpleasant to taste and certainly pleasant to look at in what is often a monochromatic salad. Although this saved the peeling step, we found the skin tended to rip when cutting the potato. Because this was especially true when the potatoes were very hot, we solved the problem in two ways. First, we cut the potatoes with a very sharp knife, which minimized ripping, and second, we found it wasn't necessary to cut them when they were hot, since warm ones are just as absorbent.

By this time we had learned that warm potatoes do absorb vinegar better than cold potatoes, but we weren't necessarily sure where we wanted the acidity: Should it be in the potato, in the dressing, or in both? After much testing, we concluded that warm potatoes can be sprinkled with two tablespoons of vinegar; add more vinegar, though, and the potatoes will taste pickled. If the salad needs more vinegar, just add it to the dressing.

Master Recipe

Boiled Potatoes for Salad

NOTE: *Potato salad starts with boiled potatoes. In our testing, we found that low-starch potatoes such as Red Bliss provide the sturdy texture needed to stand up to dressing. Baking potatoes tend to fall apart and produce a sloppy-looking salad. Make sure to cook the potatoes with their skins on to prevent them from becoming waterlogged. Cool the potatoes slightly, peel if desired, and then dress.*

2 pounds Red Bliss potatoes (about 6 medium), scrubbed

INSTRUCTIONS:

1. Place potatoes in 6-quart pot and cover with water. Bring to boil, cover, and simmer, stirring once or twice to ensure even cooking, until thin-bladed paring knife or metal cake tester inserted into a potato can be removed with no resistance, 25 to 30 minutes.

2. Drain and cool potatoes slightly. Peel if desired. Cut potatoes as directed in following recipes while still warm, rinsing knife occasionally in warm water to remove gumminess. Proceed as directed in one of the following recipes.

American-Style Potato Salad with Eggs and Sweet Pickles

serves 6 to 8

➤ NOTE: *Use sweet pickles, not relish, for the best results in this recipe.*

- 1 recipe Boiled Potatoes for Salad (page 50), cut into ¾-inch cubes
- 2 tablespoons red wine vinegar
- ½ teaspoon salt
- ½ teaspoon ground black pepper
- 3 hard-boiled eggs, peeled and cut into small dice
- 2 large scallions, sliced thin
- 1 small celery stalk, cut into small dice
- ¼ cup sweet pickles, cut into small dice
- ½ cup mayonnaise
- 2 tablespoons Dijon mustard
- ¼ cup minced fresh parsley leaves

INSTRUCTIONS:

1. Layer warm potato cubes in medium bowl, sprinkling with vinegar, salt, and pepper as you go. Refrigerate while preparing remaining ingredients.

2. Mix in remaining ingredients, adjust seasonings, and refrigerate until ready to serve, up to 1 day.

French-Style Potato Salad with Tarragon Vinaigrette

serves 6

➤ NOTE: *If fresh tarragon is not available, increase the parsley to three tablespoons and use tarragon vinegar in place of the white wine vinegar.*

- **1** **recipe Boiled Potatoes for Salad (page 50), cut into slices ¼-inch thick**
- **4** **tablespoons white wine vinegar**
- **½** **teaspoon salt**
- **½** **teaspoon ground black pepper**
- **1** **tablespoon Dijon mustard**
- **1** **medium shallot, minced**
- **6** **tablespoons extra-virgin olive oil**
- **2** **tablespoons minced fresh parsley leaves**
- **1** **tablespoon minced fresh tarragon leaves**

INSTRUCTIONS:

1. Layer warm potato slices in medium bowl, sprinkling with 2 tablespoons vinegar and salt and pepper as you go. Let stand at room temperature while preparing dressing.

2. Whisk remaining 2 tablespoons vinegar, mustard, and shallot together in small bowl. Whisk in oil so that mixture is somewhat emulsified. Pour over potatoes and toss lightly to coat. Refrigerate salad until ready to serve, up to 1 day.

3. Bring salad to room temperature, stir in parsley and tarragon, adjust seasonings, and serve.

German-Style Potato Salad with Bacon and Balsamic Vinegar

serves 6

➢ NOTE: *Smaller new potatoes are more attractive in this recipe. The slices are smaller and tend not to break up as much as those from bigger potatoes. Cider vinegar is more traditional, but we like the sweeter, fuller flavor of the balsamic vinegar.*

- **1** **recipe Boiled Potatoes for Salad (page 50), cut into slices ¼-inch thick**
- **¼** **cup balsamic or cider vinegar**
- **½** **teaspoon salt**
- **½** **teaspoon ground black pepper**
- **4–5** **slices bacon (about 4 ounces), cut crosswise into ¼-inch strips**
- **1** **medium onion, diced**
- **2** **tablespoons vegetable oil, if needed**
- **½** **cup beef broth**
- **¼** **cup minced fresh parsley leaves**

INSTRUCTIONS:

1. Layer warm potato slices in medium bowl, sprinkling with 2 tablespoons vinegar and salt and pepper as you go. Let stand at room temperature while preparing dressing.

2. Fry bacon in medium skillet over medium heat until brown and crisp, 7 to 10 minutes. Transfer bacon with slotted spoon to bowl of potatoes. Add onion to bacon drippings and sauté until softened, 4 to 5 minutes. If necessary, add oil to yield 2 tablespoons unabsorbed fat.

3. Add beef broth and bring to boil. Stir in remaining 2 tablespoons vinegar. Remove from heat and pour mixture over potatoes. Add parsley and toss gently to coat. Serve warm or tepid. (Salad may be covered and set aside at room temperature for several hours.)

Southwestern-Style Potato Salad with Chiles and Cilantro

serves 6

NOTE: *This colorful salad is moderately spicy; adjust the amounts of jalapeño and cayenne to increase or decrease the heat.*

- **1** recipe Boiled Potatoes for Salad (page 50), cut into ¾-inch cubes
- **5** tablespoons lime juice
- **½** teaspoon salt
- **½** teaspoon ground black pepper
- **1** teaspoon minced or grated lime zest
- **⅛–¼** teaspoon cayenne pepper
- **2** teaspoons ground cumin
- **1** teaspoon minced jalapeño chile
- **6** tablespoons canola oil
- **1** medium red bell pepper, cut into ¼-inch dice
- **2** tablespoons minced red onion
- **¼** cup minced fresh cilantro leaves

INSTRUCTIONS:

1. Layer warm potato cubes in medium bowl, sprinkling with 2 tablespoons lime juice and salt and pepper as you go. Let stand at room temperature while preparing dressing.

2. Combine remaining 3 tablespoons lime juice, zest, cayenne, cumin, and jalapeño in small mixing bowl. Gradually whisk in oil so that mixture is somewhat emulsified. Pour over potatoes; toss lightly to coat. Mix in bell pepper and onion. Adjust seasonings, adding cayenne and more salt, if desired. Refrigerate until ready to serve, up to 1 day.

3. Bring salad to room temperature, stir in cilantro, adjust seasonings, and serve.

Potato-Beet Salad with Horseradish and Sour Cream Dressing

serves 6

NOTE: *To simplify preparation, we wanted to cook the potatoes and beets together. We found that large potatoes and small beets will cook at the same rate and can be boiled together. Surprisingly, the beets do not stain the potatoes as long as the beets are cooked unskinned. If you must use smaller potatoes or larger beets, cook them separately.*

- 1 recipe Boiled Potatoes for Salad (page 50), made with 1 pound Red Bliss potatoes (3 medium) and 1 pound beets (5 small) with 1 inch of stem and root attached to prevent bleeding
- 2 tablespoons white vinegar
- ½ teaspoon salt
- ½ teaspoon ground black pepper
- ½ cup sour cream
- 2 tablespoons or more prepared horseradish
- 2 medium celery stalks, cut into ¼-inch dice
- 2 tablespoons minced red onion
- ¼ cup minced fresh dill leaves

INSTRUCTIONS:

1. Drain and cool potatoes and beets slightly. Peel potatoes if desired. Rub skins off beets with paper towel or your fingers and discard stems and roots. Cut potatoes and beets into quarters and then into slices ¼-inch thick while still warm, rinsing knife occasionally in warm water to remove gumminess.

2. Layer warm potato and beet slices in medium bowl, sprinkling with vinegar and salt and pepper as you go. Let stand at room temperature while preparing remaining ingredients.

3. Combine sour cream and horseradish in small bowl. Taste and add more horseradish, if desired. Mix dressing with potatoes and beets; toss lightly to coat. Mix in celery and onion. Adjust seasonings, adding more salt or a touch of vinegar if desired. Refrigerate until ready to serve, up to 1 day.

4. Bring salad to room temperature, stir in dill, adjust seasonings, and serve.

chapter seven

BOILED POTATOES

MOST OFTEN WE BOIL POTATOES FOR salad. However, freshly dug baby or new potatoes can be boiled, buttered, and served hot as a side dish.

From our initial tests we knew that having a range of sizes in the pot was problematic. The small potatoes overcooked and their skins split when cooked with larger potatoes. Use potatoes that are all the same size.

While large potatoes are fine for salad, we think that the best potatoes for boiling and buttering are small—less than 2½ inches in diameter and preferably smaller. These potatoes cooked more evenly—larger ones tended to get a bit mushy right under skin by the time the center was cooked through.

From previous tests, we knew that you must boil potatoes with their skins on to prevent them from becoming watery. However, we found that the flesh on a boiled potato must be exposed at some point so that it can soak up the butter and seasonings. When we tossed drained, whole, skin-on potatoes in a bowl with butter, the butter just stayed in the bowl—it could not penetrate the skin.

We tried peeling a thin band around the center of each potato before boiling to eliminate the need to cut them after cooking. This test failed. Once the potatoes were cooked, the skin that had been left on started to break away from the flesh, and the flesh, too, was breaking apart.

For the best flavor, we found it necessary to cut the potatoes in half after boiling. Although a bit tedious, we found that holding the hot potatoes one at a time with a pair tongs and then slicing them with a knife worked well. Once all of the potatoes were cut in half, we immediately added them to the bowl with the butter. As soon as the potatoes are coated with fat, the seasonings can be added.

Not only are cut boiled potatoes more flavorful, but they have a nicely moist mouthfeel. Comparatively, the potatoes left whole were dry and bland.

Master Recipe

Boiled Potatoes with Butter

serves 4

NOTE: *Refer to the chart on page 64 for precise cooking times for potatoes of various size. If using potatoes more than 2 inches in diameter, consider cutting them into quarters in step 3 for maximum absorption of the seasonings and ease of eating.*

3 tablespoons unsalted butter
2 pounds small Red Bliss or new potatoes, scrubbed
Salt and ground black pepper

INSTRUCTIONS:

1. Place butter in medium serving bowl and set it aside to soften while preparing and cooking potatoes.

2. Place potatoes in 6-quart pot; cover with water and add 1 tablespoon salt. Bring to a boil, cover, and simmer, stirring once or twice to ensure even cooking, until a thin-bladed paring knife or metal cake tester inserted into a potato can be removed with no resistance. Drain potatoes.

3. Cut potatoes in half, using a pair of tongs to steady hot potatoes and a sharp knife to cut them (see figure 6, page

65). Place halved potatoes in bowl with butter and toss to coat. Season with salt and pepper to taste and toss again to blend. Serve immediately.

VARIATIONS:

Boiled Potatoes with Butter and Chives

Add 3 tablespoons thinly sliced fresh chives to potatoes with salt and pepper in step 3.

Boiled Potatoes with Lemon, Parsley, and Olive Oil

Replace butter with 3 tablespoons extra-virgin olive oil. Add the minced zest of 1 lemon and 3 tablespoons chopped fresh parsley leaves to potatoes with salt and pepper in step 3.

Boiled Potatoes with Mustard, Shallots, and Tarragon

Fresh dill can be used in place of the tarragon if you prefer.

Blend 1 tablespoon Dijon mustard into butter with fork or rubber spatula once butter has softened. Add 1 tablespoon minced shallots and 2 tablespoons chopped fresh tarragon leaves to potatoes with salt and pepper in step 3.

ESTIMATED BOILING TIME FOR POTATOES

Depending on their size, small potatoes can take from 8 to 18 minutes to cook through. Use the following chart and, of course, test the potatoes with a paring knife as directed. To ensure even cooking, choose potatoes that are all the same size. The cooking time starts once the potatoes are covered and begin to simmer.

DIAMETER	NUMBER OF POTATOES IN 2 POUNDS	COOKING TIME
Less than 1 inch	32 or more	8 to 10 minutes
1 to 1½ inches	25 to 31	10 to 12 minutes
1½ to 2 inches	18 to 24	12 to 15 minutes
2 to 2½ inches	12 to 17	15 to 18 minutes

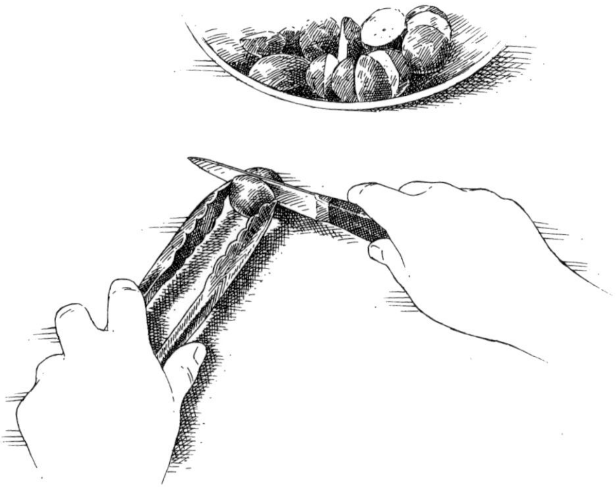

Figure 6.
Potatoes should be boiled whole and unpeeled so that they don't become soggy. After boiling, however, the potatoes should be cut in half, because the fleshy portion of the potato absorbs butter and seasonings far better than the skin. Steady the hot potato with a pair of tongs while cutting it with a sharp knife.

chapter eight

SAUTÉED POTATOES

CRISP SLICES OR CHUNKS OF SAUTÉED POTATOES (often called home fries) are a breakfast favorite. They also make an excellent side dish for dinner. Some recipes suggest that potatoes can be sautéed without precooking. Most sources, however, start by boiling or baking potatoes and then sautéing to get them crisp. We started with questions about the potatoes (the type, whether or not they should be peeled, whether to slice or dice) and then moved on to test various cooking methods.

Yukon Golds were the clear favorites in our testing. They produced home fries with a rich golden color and crisp exterior. Starchier russet potatoes fell apart in our tests and are not recommended. Red potatoes are fine but could not match the Yukon Golds in terms of appearance or flavor.

All of our testers preferred the texture and flavor that the skin added, so we decided not to peel potatoes for home fries. We found that sliced potatoes were much harder to cook than diced potatoes. A pound of sliced potatoes stacks up three or four layers deep in a large skillet, and the result is uneven cooking, with some potatoes burned and others undercooked. Potatoes cut into ½-inch dice brown much more evenly. We found that a 12-inch skillet can hold 1¼ pounds of diced potatoes in a single layer.

In our tests, raw potatoes, no matter how small they were cut, burned before the interior had cooked sufficiently. We decided to precook the potatoes before sautéing.

We started by dicing baked potatoes and found the texture gummy and the exterior not terribly crisp. Potatoes that were boiled until tender and then diced broke down in the pan, and the inside was overcooked by the time the exterior was crisp. We tried braising diced potatoes, figuring we could cook them through in a covered pan with some water and fat, remove the cover, let the water evaporate, and then crisp up the potatoes in the remaining fat. Although this sounds like a good idea, each time the potatoes stuck horribly to the pan.

The best results occurred when we boiled diced potatoes briefly, drained them, and then sautéed them. Since the potatoes were drained once the water came to a boil, they didn't absorb much water and held their shape nicely.

We think potatoes taste best when sautéed in butter, but a combination of oil and butter is much easier to work with and far less likely to burn. We particularly liked the combination of corn oil and butter, but peanut oil, canola oil, or olive oil can be used in place of corn oil.

Master Recipe

Sautéed Potatoes

serves 3 to 4

NOTE: *The potatoes must be cooked in a pan large enough to hold them in a single layer. A 12-inch skillet will do the job. Use a spatula to turn the potatoes as they cook. Work gently so that you don't break the crisp crust that forms on the side cooking against the pan bottom.*

- **1¼ pounds Yukon Gold potatoes, scrubbed and cut into ½-inch cubes**
- **1¼ teaspoons salt**
- **1½ tablespoons corn oil**
- **1½ tablespoons unsalted butter**
- **⅛ teaspoon ground black pepper**

INSTRUCTIONS:

1. Place potatoes in 6-quart pot; cover with water and add 1 teaspoon salt. Bring to a boil over medium-high heat. As soon as water begins to boil, drain potatoes well.

2. Heat oil and butter in heavy-bottomed large skillet over medium-high heat until butter foams. Add potatoes and shake pan so that potatoes form a single layer. When potatoes are golden brown on bottom (after about 4 minutes), carefully use a wooden spatula to turn them. Continue cooking potatoes, turning them three or four more times, until nicely browned on all sides, about 15 to 20 minutes in total. Season with remaining ¼ teaspoon salt and pepper to taste and stir. Serve immediately or keep warm in preheated 300-degree oven for up to 20 minutes.

VARIATIONS:

Sautéed Potatoes with Rosemary and Garlic

Replace corn oil and butter with 3 tablespoons extra-virgin olive oil. When potatoes are browned on all sides, add 2 teaspoons chopped fresh rosemary and 1 teaspoon minced garlic. Cook for another 2 to 3 minutes over low heat, shaking pan frequently to coat potatoes with rosemary and garlic and to cook garlic. Season with salt and pepper and serve.

Home Fries

While potatoes are being blanched, heat 1 tablespoon corn oil in large, heavy-bottomed skillet. Add 1 medium onion, chopped fine, and sauté over medium-high heat until lightly browned, 8 to 10 minutes. Scrape onions into bowl. Add 1½ tablespoons oil and 1½ tablespoons butter to empty pan as directed in step 2. Cook potatoes as directed. When potatoes are browned all over, return onions to pan along with 1 teaspoon paprika and stir to coat. Season with salt and pepper as directed and serve.

Spicy Home Fries

Follow Home Fries variation, adding a pinch or two of cayenne pepper to potatoes along with paprika.

Home Fries with Bell Pepper and Cumin

Follow Home Fries variation, cooking 1 finely chopped red or green bell pepper with onion. Remove pepper with onion and add back to pan along with paprika and 1 teaspoon ground cumin. Season with salt and pepper as directed and serve.

chapter nine

HASH BROWNS

HASH BROWNS ARE BEST DEFINED AS THIN, crisp sautéed potato cakes made with grated or chopped potatoes, raw or precooked. We tested various kinds of potatoes and found high-starch russets to yield the best results overall. They adhered well, browned beautifully, and had the most pronounced potato flavor.

Our next challenge was to decide between raw and precooked potatoes. Precooked potatoes tasted good, but when chopped they did not stay together in a cohesive cake, and when grated they needed to be pressed very hard to form a cake. Unfortunately, this meant they ended up having the mouthfeel of fried mashed potato. Although this is an acceptable alternative if you have leftover cooked potatoes, we preferred using raw, grated potatoes. We also liked the more textured interior, the pronounced potato taste, and the way the raw shreds of potatoes formed an attractive, deeply browned crust.

Choosing the best method for cutting the potatoes was easy. In our tests, chopped potatoes never stayed together in the pan. No matter how finely diced, they were simply chopped, sautéed potatoes, not hash browns. Grating the potatoes on the large-hole side of a box grater or with the shredding disk on a food processor yielded hash browns that formed a coherent cake when cooked.

After cooking countless batches of hash browns, we found that the pan itself was an important factor. A skillet with sloping sides makes it considerably easier to press the potatoes into a flattened shape, invert them, and slide them from the pan. All of these tasks were difficult in a straight-sided frying pan. Uncoated stainless steel pans produced the best crust, but nonstick pans provided adequate browning and are far easier to clean.

Hash browns can be made into one or more individual servings or one large portion that can be cut into wedges. If making a single cake, fold it over just before serving so that each wedge of hash brown has four (not just two) crisp edges. No matter how you choose to present the hash browns, make sure you serve them steaming hot.

Master Recipe

Hash Browns

serves 3 to 4

➢ NOTE: *To prevent potatoes from turning brown, grate them just before cooking. For individual servings, simply divide the grated potatoes into four equal portions and reduce cooking time to 5 minutes per side. To vary flavor, add 2 tablespoons grated onion, 1 to 2 tablespoons herb of choice, or roasted garlic to taste to the raw grated potatoes. You can also garnish the cooked hash browns with snipped chives or scallion tops just before serving.*

1 pound russet potatoes, peeled, washed, and dried
¼ teaspoon salt
Ground black pepper
1 tablespoon unsalted butter

INSTRUCTIONS:

1. Using shredding disk of food processor or large holes on box grater, coarsely grate potatoes. Wrap grated potatoes in clean kitchen towel and squeeze dry (see figure 7, page 76). Toss fully dried grated potatoes (you should have about 1½ cups) with salt and pepper to taste in medium bowl.

2. Meanwhile, heat half the butter in a 10-inch skillet over medium-high heat until it just starts to brown, then scatter potatoes evenly over entire pan bottom. Using wide spatula, firmly press potatoes to flatten; reduce heat to medium and continue cooking until dark golden brown and crisp, 7 to 8 minutes.

3. Invert hash browns, browned-side up, onto large plate; add remaining butter to pan. Once butter has melted, slide hash browns back into pan. Continue to cook over medium heat until second side is dark golden brown and crisp, 5 to 6 minutes longer.

4. Fold potato round in half (see figure 8, page 77) and cook 1 minute longer. Slide hash browns onto plate or cutting board, cut into wedges, and serve immediately.

VARIATION:

Hash Browns with Smoked Cheddar and Herbs

Add 1½ teaspoons each minced fresh parsley, dill, and chives to grated potatoes in step 1. Cook as directed. After second side has turned dark brown and crisp in step 3, cover half of cake with ¼ cup shredded smoked cheddar. Continue with step 4, folding uncovered half of cake over cheese-covered half. Cook until cheese melts, about 2 minutes. Serve immediately.

Figure 7.
To release the water from the grated potatoes, place them in a towel, and, using two hands, twist the towel tightly to squeeze out as much moisture as possible.

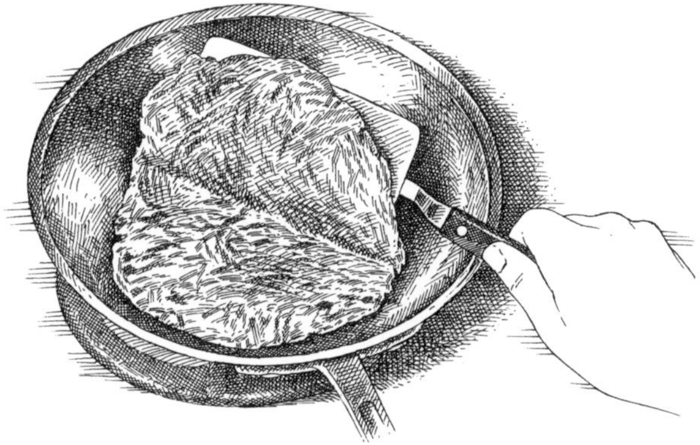

Figure 8.
Just before serving, fold the large flat hash brown cake over, omelet style. When cut into wedges, each piece will then have four crisp edges.

chapter ten

LATKES

LATKES ARE THICK, GRATED POTATO PANcakes that are pan-fried in vegetable oil. They should be golden and very crisp on the exterior, creamy and moist on the interior.

We tested russets, red potatoes, and Yukon Golds. The russet potato pancakes had a pleasantly pronounced potato flavor and dry texture. The red potato pancakes were at the other end of the spectrum; very creamy, almost gluey on the side. The Yukon Gold pancakes were an attractive yellow-gold color, tasted somewhat sweet and mild, and were creamy in texture but not gluey at all. The pancakes made with Yukon Gold potatoes were deemed the best, followed closely by the pancakes made with the russets.

In our tests, we found that most latke recipes produce pancakes that are either thick and creamy or thin and crisp. We wanted a thick pancake with a creamy center, but the exterior had to be lacy and crisp

Shredded potatoes make latkes that are very crisp and lacy on the exterior. For a creamier interior, we found it best to grind the potatoes to a coarse puree. We decided to use both shredded and more finely grated potatoes. We simply took some of the shredded potatoes out of the food processor and pulsed those remaining (with the onion added) until pretty fine. This two-step procedure gave us the best of both worlds: latkes with an exterior that cooked up crisp because of the larger shred and an interior that was thick and chewy, like a traditional pancake.

Many recipes use a lot of flour or matzo meal as a binder. These starches help soak up some of the moisture the cut potatoes exude. Unfortunately, starches can make latkes heavy. We decide to press out some of the moisture by hand and then lightly bind the potatoes with the starch that settles to the bottom of the bowl filled with the potato water.

We found the temperature of the oil to be crucial to frying the perfect latkes. Unfortunately, there's not enough oil in the pan to use a thermometer. Instead, you must look for visual clues. When the oil is hot enough for frying, it will shimmer on the surface and look kind of wavy.

Latkes

makes fourteen 3-inch pancakes

NOTE: *Matzo meal is a traditional binder, though we found that the pancake was neither improved nor harmed by the addition of this ingredient in small amounts. Applesauce and sour cream are the classic accompaniments for latkes. This recipe will serve four to six people.*

2 pounds Yukon Gold or russet potatoes, peeled
1 medium onion, peeled and cut into eighths
1 large egg
4 medium scallions, white and green parts, minced
3 tablespoons minced fresh parsley leaves
2 tablespoons matzo meal (optional)
1½ teaspoons salt
Ground black pepper
1 cup vegetable oil for frying

INSTRUCTIONS:

1. Grate potatoes in food processor fitted with shredding blade. Place half the potatoes in fine mesh sieve set over medium bowl and reserve. Fit food processor with metal blade, add onion, and pulse with remaining potatoes until all pieces measure roughly ⅛ inch and look coarsely chopped, 5 to 6 one-second pulses. Mix with reserved potato shreds in sieve and press against sieve to drain as much liquid as possible into bowl below. Let potato liquid in bowl stand until starch settles to bottom, about 1 minute. Pour off liquid, leaving starch in bowl. Beat egg, the potato mixture, and remaining ingredients except oil into starch.

2. Heat ¼-inch depth of oil in large skillet over medium-high heat until shimmering but not smoking. Working one at a time, place ¼ cup potato mixture, squeezed of excess liquid and pressed into a disc ½ inch thick, in oil. Press gently with nonstick spatula; repeat until 5 latkes are in pan.

3. Maintaining heat so fat bubbles around edges of latkes, fry until golden brown on bottom and edges, about 3 minutes. Turn with spatula and continue frying until golden brown all over, about 3 minutes more. Drain on triple thickness of paper towels set on wire rack over jelly roll pan. Repeat with remaining potato mixture, returning oil to temperature between each batch and replacing oil after second batch. (Cooled latkes can be covered loosely with plastic wrap, held at room temperature for 4 hours, transferred to a heated cookie sheet, and baked in a 375-degree oven until crisp and hot, about 5 minutes). Season with salt and pepper to taste and serve immediately.

chapter eleven

POTATO GRATIN

A POTATO GRATIN—ALSO KNOWN AS SCALLOPED potatoes—consists of thinly sliced potatoes covered by a liquid and baked in a wide, shallow baking pan until the potatoes are tender and the top gets a burnished crust. Most recipes follow the same procedure: Rub an ovenproof dish with garlic, brush it with butter, layer it with sliced potatoes, add seasonings and just enough liquid to cover the potatoes, and bake.

We tried all the major potato varieties, including all-purpose whites, boilers, yellow-fleshed, and new potatoes. All made tasty gratins, but we did find subtle variations in flavor and texture—waxy potatoes ended up firmer, for example, while floury baking potatoes were more tender. However, the differences were relatively slight, and we began to suspect that the way the potato is sliced is more significant than which type is used.

We found that potatoes cut into 1/16-inch slices soaked up the cooking liquid and melted into a cakelike texture. When sliced 1/8-inch thick, however, they kept their shape nicely throughout baking but still melded together. When sliced too thick (1/4 inch or more), however, the potato slices did not properly meld together in the oven. Don't slice potatoes in advance and hold them in water. We found that this caused their starch to leech out, resulting in a bland gratin with layers that do not hold together properly.

The pan in which you make a gratin is an important consideration. A standard gratin dish is oval, 10 to 12 inches long, and 6 to 8 inches wide. As it turns out, the dimensions of the pan are more important than the material it's made of. We cooked successful gratins in a variety of dishes, from classic enamel to earthenware to ovenproof glass—the key is that they were all shallow. Two to three layers of potatoes should come about three quarters of the way up the sides of the pan so they cook evenly and have a broad surface area to brown.

We found 350 degrees to be the best oven temperature. At higher temperatures, the slices on the top of the gratin tended to dry out and become tough. We also discovered that it helps to baste the top slices once or twice during the cooking so they stay moist and brown evenly.

We made gratins using a variety of liquids, including whole milk, low-fat milk, half-and-half, heavy cream, meat broths, and water. The heavy cream had a tendency to break up and become greasy, particularly at higher temperatures. The low-fat milk, on the other hand, was insipid, while the whole milk was almost completely soaked up by the potatoes, leaving only a light curd between the layers. Our favorite all-purpose dairy cooking medium turned out to be half-and-half. The gratins we made with it had just the right balance of saturated potato and saucy liquid, without overwhelming the taste of the potato. They were also easy to prepare.

Until this point, we had tried pouring cold liquids over the layered potatoes and baking them. We wondered if we could cut the cooking time by heating the potatoes and liquid beforehand. We placed a pound of sliced potatoes, enough liquid to barely cover them, salt, and pepper into a saucepan and brought the liquid to a boil, stirring occasionally so the potatoes didn't scorch or stick. We next lowered the heat and simmered the mixture until the liquid thickened. Finally, we poured the potatoes into a baking dish and finished them in a 350-degree oven.

This method proved to possess many benefits. The cooking time was reduced, the assembly of the gratin took less time, and, because the seasoning was added to the liquid, the final product was evenly seasoned.

There are several ways to enhance the crust from which these dishes get their name (the French word gratin means "crust"). Dotting the top with butter makes for a golden crust, as does cheese. A nice finish can also be achieved by pouring a thin layer of cream over the top of the gratin for the final 20 or 30 minutes of baking. This cap of cream browns evenly without greasy edges.

Potato Gratin

serves 4 to 6

➢ NOTE: *Russet potatoes will produce a more tender gratin; slices of waxy new potatoes will be firmer. Use either, depending on your personal preference. For a more pronounced crust, sprinkle three tablespoons of heavy cream or grated Gruyère cheese on top of the potatoes after 45 minutes of baking. A mandolin or V-slicer will make quick work of the potatoes, but a sharp chef's knife can be used if you prefer.*

1 large garlic clove, peeled and smashed
1 tablespoon unsalted butter, softened
2¼ cups half-and-half
1¼ teaspoons salt
⅛ teaspoon ground black pepper
Pinch grated nutmeg
Pinch cayenne pepper (optional)
2 pounds potatoes, peeled and sliced ⅛-inch thick

INSTRUCTIONS:

1. Adjust oven rack to center position and heat oven to 350 degrees. Rub bottom and sides of 5- to 6-cup gratin dish or shallow baking dish with garlic. Mince remaining garlic and set aside. Once garlic in dish has dried, about 2 minutes, spread dish with half the butter.

2. Bring half-and-half, salt, pepper, nutmeg, cayenne (if desired), potatoes, and reserved garlic to boil in medium saucepan over medium-high heat, stirring occasionally with wooden spoon (liquid will just barely cover potatoes). Reduce heat and simmer until liquid thickens, about 2 minutes.

3. Pour potato mixture into prepared dish; shake dish or use fork to distribute potatoes evenly. Gently press down on potatoes until submerged in liquid; dot with remaining butter.

4. Bake until top is golden brown (basting once or twice during first 45 minutes), about 75 minutes. Let rest 10 minutes and serve.

chapter twelve

SWEET POTATOES

SWEET POTATOES, OFTEN MISLABELED AS YAMS IN markets (a yam is actually a huge tropical tuber covered with thick, brown skin), come in two distinct types—dry and moist. Dry sweet potatoes have white-to-yellow flesh, while moist ones have orange flesh. The second variety appears more often in markets.

Dry sweet potatoes are slightly sweet and mealy, almost like a russet potato. Moist sweet potatoes have a higher sugar content and are dense, watery, and more easily caramelized. Neither variety should be washed until just before cooking, as sweet potatoes have thin skins that can go soft very easily. Refrigeration is a no-no; it causes the flesh to soften and promotes the growth of mold. Store sweet potatoes in a cool, dark, well-ventilated spot.

Master Recipe

Sweet Potato Casserole

serves 8 to 12

➢ NOTE: *Most holiday sweet potato casseroles are too sweet and swimming in butter. This casserole is sweet but not cloying, rich but not fatty. In our tests, we found that parboiling the sweet potatoes is essential. It sets their bright orange color and releases their sugars. Casseroles made with potatoes that were not pre-cooked were dry and less flavorful.*

- 3 pounds sweet potatoes (about 6 medium), peeled, halved lengthwise, and halves cut crosswise into ¼-inch slices
- 6 tablespoons unsalted butter, melted, plus softened butter for baking dish
- 2 tablespoons honey
- 3 tablespoons molasses
- 1 tablespoon grated fresh gingerroot or 1 teaspoon ground ginger
- ¾ teaspoon salt
- ¼ teaspoon cayenne pepper
- 1½ tablespoons cornstarch

INSTRUCTIONS:

1. Adjust oven rack to middle position and heat oven to 375 degrees. Bring several quarts of water to boil in large pot, add sweet potato slices, and boil over high heat until sweet potatoes are bright orange and the point of a paring knife easily pierces but does not break apart a few slices, 4 to 5 minutes. Drain potatoes well and turn into buttered 13 by 9-inch dish.

2. Whisk melted butter, honey, molasses, ginger, salt, and cayenne in small bowl; set aside. Mix cornstarch with 2 tablespoons cold water in small bowl until totally smooth, then whisk into butter mixture. Pour butter mixture over sweet potatoes and toss to coat well.

3. Cover dish tightly with foil and bake until liquid is bubbly, about 50 minutes. Remove foil, stir potatoes gently, and bake until liquid thickens to glaze potatoes, about 20 minutes. Cool slightly and serve hot or at room temperature.

VARIATIONS:

Sweet Potato Casserole with Maple

Follow recipe for Sweet Potato Casserole, substituting 5 tablespoons maple syrup for honey and molasses.

Sweet Potato Casserole with Orange

Follow recipe for Sweet Potato Casserole, adding 4 teaspoons finely grated orange zest to butter mixture.

Sweet Potato Casserole with Lemon and Bourbon

Follow recipe for Sweet Potato Casserole, adding 3 tablespoons lemon juice to butter mixture and substituting ¼ cup bourbon for water in cornstarch mixture.

Sweet Potato Casserole with Pecan Topping

Much sweeter than the original recipe, but delicious.

Stir together 6 tablespoons light brown sugar and ¼ cup flour in small bowl. Add 4 tablespoons cold butter, cut into ¼-inch pieces, and toss to coat. Pinch between fingertips until mixture is crumbly and resembles coarse cornmeal. Stir in ½ cup chopped pecans; cover and refrigerate until needed. Follow recipe for Sweet Potato Casserole, sprinkling cold nut mixture over potatoes after removing foil. Proceed as directed, baking until topping is crisp and dark golden brown, about 20 minutes.

Master Recipe

Baked Sweet Potatoes

serves 4

NOTE: *The skin on baked sweet potatoes can be tough and unappealing, We found that lightly coating the skin with oil softens it slightly and promotes caramelization. This recipe is designed for the orange-flesh varieties of sweet potato that generally show up in supermarkets. If you have white-fleshed sweet potatoes, increase the baking time by about 10 minutes and use plenty of butter to moisten their drier flesh.*

- **4 medium sweet potatoes (about 2 pounds), scrubbed, dried, and lightly pricked with a fork**
- **2 tablespoons vegetable or olive oil**
- **Salt and ground black pepper**
- **Unsalted butter**

INSTRUCTIONS:

1. Adjust oven rack to center position and heat oven to 400 degrees. Rub potatoes with oil, then arrange on foil-lined baking sheet as far apart as possible.

2. Bake until knife tip slips easily into potato center, 40 to 50 minutes. Remove sweet potatoes from oven and pierce with a fork to create a dotted X (see figure 1, page 18). Press in at ends of sweet potato to push flesh up and out (see figure 2, page 18). Season with salt and pepper to taste. Dot with butter to taste and serve.

VARIATION:

Mashed Sweet Potatoes

Bake sweet potatoes as directed. As soon as they come out of the oven, remove peels and put sweet potatoes through a ricer or food mill, pressing the tiny bits into a medium bowl. (You can use a potato masher to mash the peeled potatoes in a bowl, but the texture will be coarse and not nearly as silky.) Stir in 5 tablespoons softened butter and salt and pepper to taste. Beat with a spoon until silky and smooth.

Master Recipe

Oven-Fried Sweet Potatoes

serves 4

NOTE: *Make sure to handle sweet potatoes with a thin metal spatula in the oven. You need to loosen them carefully from the baking sheet so that the crusty exterior does not rip or stick to the pan.*

4 teaspoons peanut oil
2 pound sweet potatoes (3 large), scrubbed
Salt and ground black pepper

INSTRUCTIONS:

1. Place ½ teaspoon oil on each of two rimmed baking sheets. Use paper towel to spread oil evenly over entire surface and place both sheets in oven. Preheat oven to 400 degrees.

2. Cut each sweet potato from end to end into eight thick wedges. Toss sweet potatoes and remaining tablespoon of oil in medium bowl to coat; season generously with salt and pepper to taste and toss again to blend. Carefully remove one baking sheet from oven and place half of sweet potatoes on baking sheet cut-side down; spread them out so they do not touch each other. Place baking sheet back in oven and repeat process using second baking sheet and remaining sweet potatoes.

3. Bake until cut side of sweet potato touching baking sheet is crusty and golden brown, 15 to 20 minutes. Remove from oven and carefully turn sweet potatoes, using a metal spatula to loosen them from baking sheet. Bake until second cut side of sweet potato now touching pan is crusty and golden brown, 10 to 15 minutes. Use metal spatula to transfer sweet potatoes to platter and serve immediately.

VARIATION:

Sweet Potato Oven Fries with Indian Spices

Combine 1 teaspoon ground turmeric, 1 teaspoon ground coriander, ½ teaspoon ground cumin, and 1½ teaspoons curry powder in small bowl. Add spice mixture to potatoes along with salt and pepper in step 2.

index